Consultant Penny Brooke
Managing Editor Belinda Hollyer
Editor Philip Steele
Design Jane Robison
  Sally Boothroyd
Picture Research Suzanne Williams
Production Rosemary Bishop
Illustrations Raymond Turvey
Maps Matthews & Taylor Associates/
  Swanston Graphics (pages 44–45)

Photographic Sources Key to positions of illustrations: (T) top, (C) centre, (B) bottom, (L) left, (R) right

Associated Press: 22(T) BBC Hulton Picture Library: 16(T), 17(TR), 19(TL,TR,CR), 34(CR) British Museum: 14(C) British Petroleum: 25(BR) Camera Press: 21(BL) Camerapix Hutchison Library: 9(B) Leslie Woodhead, 30(L) Felix Greene, 35(B)&36(T) Michael MacIntyre, 39(BL) Felix Greene, 41(B) Lynn Turner; Tim Canadine: 6–7, 9(T), 12–13(T), 27(CR), 29(TL,BR), 32(BR), 33(B), 35(TR), 37(BL) Chinese Visual Aids Project, Faculty of Languages, Polytechnic of Central London: endpapers, 8–9(T), 10(CT), 12(B), 21(BR), 28(L), 31(TL), 34(CL), 37(TL,TR,BR) Keystone Press Agency/Photo Source: 21(TR) Royal Scottish Museum, Edinburgh, Crown copyright reserved: 14(BR) Sonia Halliday Photographs: 14(T), 15(L) Robert Harding Picture Library: 8(TL,B), 11(B), 23(T), 24(B), 26–7, 27(TR,B), 28–9, 29(TR), 32(BL), 33(TR), 36(B), 38(R), 40–1(T), 41(TR) Mansell Collection: 13(B), 17(BR), 18(T) Mary Evans Picture Library: 14(BL), 16–17 Productions Television Rencontre: 15(R), 18(B) Rex Features: 22(C), 23(B), Snark International: 16(BL) Society for Anglo-Chinese Understanding: 10(CR,BL,BR), 10–11(T), 20–1, 22–3, 24–5(T,B), 25(TR), 31(TR), 32(T), 33(TL), 34–5(T), 38(L), 39(T,BR), ZEFA: 10(CL), 31(B), 40(B)

A MACDONALD BOOK

First published in Great Britain in 1974 by Macdonald Educational Ltd

This revised edition published in 1986 by Macdonald & Co (Publishers) Ltd London & Sydney A BPCC plc company

Printed and bound in Great Britain by Purnell Book Production Ltd

Macdonald & Co (Publishers) Ltd
Greater London House
Hampstead Road
London NW1 7QX

British Library Cataloguing in Publication [
Merton, Anna
  China.—(Countries)
  1. China—History
  I. Title   II. Kan, Shio-yun   III. Serie
  951   DS735

ISBN 0-356-11510-0
ISBN 0-356-11511-9 Pbk

China

the land and its people

Anna Merton
and
Shio-yun Kan

Macdonald Educational

Contents

A vast country

China is a huge country, as you will see from the maps at the end of the book. It covers an area of nearly 9,600,000 square kilometres, and is divided into 29 provinces, municipalities and 'autonomous' (partly self-governing) regions. Tibet (Xizang) in the southwest, and Xinjiang, in the northwest, are examples of the latter.

China is less than half the size of its powerful neighbour, the Soviet Union, but it has the world's largest population, over 1,000 million. Most people live on the fertile plains and hills of central and eastern China.

Much of China, however, is made up of harsher terrain. The world's highest peak, Mt Everest (8,848 metres), lies in the Himalayan range on China's border with Nepal. Its Tibetan name is Qomolangma. There are also vast tracts of desert, such as the Taklamakan and the Gobi. Some areas of China are in earthquake zones.

The two greatest rivers run eastwards to the sea from the western mountains. In the north is the Huang He, or 'Yellow River'. It is sometimes referred to as 'China's sorrow', because of the destruction it has caused over thousands of years by flooding and silting. To the south is the Yangzi Jiang, also known as the Chang Jiang, or 'Long River'. Both of these rivers are now being dammed, dyked and controlled, to provide water for hydroelectric power and irrigation.

Climate and crops

In northern China, water is scarcer. Here the winters are dry, cold and often dusty, whilst the summers are hot, with occasional outbursts of rain. The main crop is winter wheat, which people use to make noodles and steamed buns, their staple food.

In the warm, rainy, frost-free south, rice has been grown as the staple food for some 7,000 years. Cotton is grown in the Huang He basin and in the lower Yangzi Jiang plain, as well as in Xinjiang. Silk is produced over much of the country nowadays, particularly in the provinces of Zhejiang, Jiangsu, Sichuan and Guangdong. The south is important for one of China's most famous products, tea.

▲ Vegetable fields near Guangzhou (Canton) in southern China. Vegetable-producing areas are often to be found close to cities and towns, and the water buffalo is indispensable in the wet fields of the south. Fields with irrigation channels are known as 'wet fields', whilst 'paddy fields' are completely flooded for part of the year.

▲ This small, traditional pavilion is bein renovated. It overlooks the mighty Huan He, or Yellow River. For thousands of years the plains of the Huang He Basin have been flooded by the river, which ha left behind the yellow 'loess' soil for whi the area is famous. Navigable sections of the river need constant dredging.

▼ The Li Jiang flows through Guilin in southeast China. The extraordinary 'kars mountains of Guilin attract tourists from China and overseas. Many fishermen in the region live permanently on boats wit their families. They are famous for using cormorants for fishing. These diving bir are attached to lines.

▲ Northern China is not very fertile, and the mountains and hillsides are often bare of trees. It is less densely populated than the south, and peoples' incomes are generally lower. Northerners have less access to good communications and to the advantages of city life.

▼ The chief river of Shanghai is the Huang Pu, which flows into the Yangzi Jiang. The Shanghai waterfront, known as the Bund, was built in the late nineteenth century. It enabled large ships to moor in the centre of the city. This area used to be under British control.

The peoples of China

China is a country of many different peoples: there are in fact fifty-six ethnic minorities. However most of the people we think of as being typically Chinese belong to the Han group, which forms ninety-four percent of the population. There are Han Chinese in every part of the country, so not surprisingly they too have regional differences in their way of life.

Language

The official language of China is 'Standard Chinese' or Mandarin. But Han Chinese people in Shanghai and Guangzhou (Canton) and in the areas between these two cities speak their own languages, which sound as different from standard Chinese as French and German do from English. Han Chinese people in those parts of China other than the southeast speak dialects of standard Chinese rather than distinct languages.

The Chinese languages are spoken in many parts of the world. Traders and workmen left southeast China as early as the sixteenth and seventeenth centuries, and large numbers of labourers also left in the nineteenth century. Southeast Asia, the Americas, Mauritius, Australia and Europe have all seen the growth of Chinese communities. The languages commonly spoken by overseas Chinese include Teochiu, from the Shantou (Swatow) area; Hokkien, from the area round the cities of Quanzhou and Xiamen (Amoy); Cantonese, from the Guangzhou area; Hakka, from the area north of Guangzhou and Shantou; and Shanghainese.

The Chinese language is 'tonal': the voice rises or falls on the various sounds of the language, and different tones can give the same sound various meanings. In standard Chinese there are four tones, which can give the sound 'ma' completely different meanings. *Mā* means 'mother', whilst *má* means 'hemp'; *mǎ* means 'horse' and *mà* 'to scold'. You can see that if you use the wrong tone it can lead to serious misunderstandings! In many dialects of Chinese, tones as well as pronunciation can vary from the standard version.

Despite these differences, the Han Chinese languages are all written in the same way. The script is made up of characters or 'ideograms', each of which represents a sound of one syllable and has its own meaning.

▲ A woman makes an offering of butter Lhasa's Jokhang monastery. Lhasa, capi of Tibet, is the centre of Lamaist Buddhism. The butter is made from yak' milk and used in Tibetan lamps as well a being mixed into Tibetan tea.

▲ Some of China's many ethnic groups The Mongolian woman (1) belongs to a nomadic people. Traditionally, Mongolians live in felt tents called 'yurts Nowadays many live in Chinese-style villages. The Han Chinese woman (2) wears a plain jacket, but many young people today prefer western fashions. Th Uighurs (3) often live in the towns and oases of the Xinjiang Autonomous Regi They are famous for carpet-making, and cultivate melons and grapes. Other Turk peoples in the region live in the hills and raise sheep. Miao people (4) retain many of their traditions. Their communities are scattered through southern China. Handicrafts are the main industry in Tibe This Tibetan (5) makes silver bowls.

Ethnic Groups of China

Uninhabited areas	
Dai	
Tungusic	
Uighur (Turkic)	Korean
Kazakh (Turkic)	Han (Chinese)
Tadzhik (Indo-European)	Miao-Yao
Mongolian	Tibetan and Tibeto-Burman
Mon-Khmer	▲ Hui (Chinese Moslems who speak Chinese)

Members of ethnic minorities
normally learn standard Chinese at
school, and from the radio and
television, but they also speak their
own distinct languages.

Although there are minority
communities in every part of China,
they are mostly found in the border
regions, often in difficult mountainous
terrain, or in remote pastoral areas.

Beliefs and customs

Members of the minority nationalities
are allowed by the Chinese
government to follow their own
religions, within certain limits. The
Tibetans believe in a form of
Buddhism. The Turkic peoples of
Xinjiang are largely Moslem.

Socialist China is officially an
atheist, Marxist state, in which
religion does not play an important
part. Even so, there are in China today
many who practise Christianity and
Buddhism, and some who follow
Taoism, an ancient Chinese religion.

Traditional festivals are still
celebrated enthusiastically. The
Chinese Lunar New Year falls in
January or February each year. The
Dragon Boat festival is in June, and in
the mid-autumn festival 'moon-cakes'
are eaten. The state festivals of May
Day and National Day (October 1)
are also important occasions.

▲ This map shows where the different
peoples of China come from, or where
they have settled. Because of their
different ways of life, minority ethnic
groups have sometimes been looked
down on by the Han Chinese.

▼ Dragon dancers weave through the
streets in celebration of the Chinese New
Year, also known as the 'Spring Festival'.
Dragons signify wealth. Most New Year
celebrations are centred upon the home,
with eating, chatting and card-playing.

Ancient China

The yellow soil (or 'loess') found in the river basin of the Huang He is ideal for farming, and it attracted settlement in ancient times. Chinese civilization is one of the oldest in the world, dating back over 3,000 years.

Over the centuries, Chinese culture was sometimes influenced by that of its neighbours. In the first century AD, for example, the Buddhist religion came into China from India.

Traditionally, however, China saw itself as the centre of the world, and other races and nations as inferior. The Chinese word for China is *Zhong Guo*, which means 'central kingdom'. Chinese culture was so powerful that most invaders, regarded by the Chinese as 'barbarians', soon adapted to the Chinese way of life.

Imperial rule
In its early stages, China was just a collection of small states which were often at war with each other. In 221 BC they were unified for the first time under one emperor, Qin Shihuang. This ruler followed the beliefs of a group of philosophers who favoured a strict, centralized organisation of the state.

It was however the ideas of another philosopher, Confucius, who had lived in the fifth century BC, which were to influence many later emperors (or 'sons of heaven', as they were known). According to Confucius, rulers and government officials needed to study the classical philosophical writings of ancient China. A balanced and stable society depended upon subordination. This meant that women had to obey men, children had to obey their fathers, and the people had to obey the scholars who acted as local officials.

China achieved a great deal in the world of politics, technology and the arts, until well into the Ming dynasty (1368–1644). However the Confucian influence upon education and administration did not help. It stressed book-learning and traditional values rather than coming to terms with the problems of the day.

In 1644 the Manchurians, from the northeast, conquered China and founded the Qing dynasty. Under the later Manchurian rulers, China was plunged into a long period of chaos.

◀ China developed its own unique civilization at a very early stage. Remains of an early type of human (*Homo erectus*) were found at Zhou Kou Dian, a famous archaeological site near Beijing. This 'Peking Man' lived over 500,000 years ago

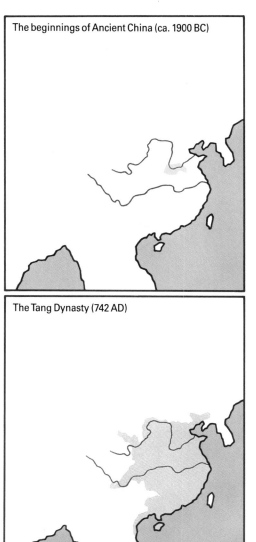

The beginnings of Ancient China (ca. 1900 BC)

The Qin Dynasty (ca. 221 BC)

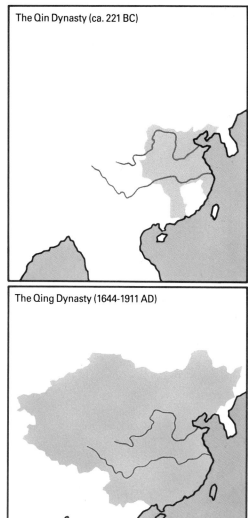

The Tang Dynasty (742 AD)

The Qing Dynasty (1644-1911 AD)

The Great Wall of China is the only
ct made by humans visible from the
n. It is 3,460 kilometres long. During
Warring States period (403 – 221 BC)
ral states built defensive earthworks
ykes to protect themselves from each
r or from the warlike non-Chinese
le of the north. It was Qin Shihuang,
irst emperor, who linked together
y of these walls into one formidable
of defence.

enghis Khan was a Mongol who
ed the tribes of the Central Asian
pe in 1206, and conquered part of
h China in 1215. His grandson Kublai
completed the Mongol domination
hina by 1280, but adopted the Chinese
tutions. He also ruled a huge part of
tral Asia.

his ghostly army is made up of
cotta figures dug out of the yellow
s soil near Xi'an in recent years.
usands of these soldiers guarded the
b of the first emperor, Qin Shihuang,
each face was sculpted with a different
ession. Model horses and chariots
also buried. The emperor's tomb
f has still to be excavated, but it is
ted to be full of riches.

13

Inventions and influence

Chinese technology and basic science were well in advance of western nations until the seventeenth century. Early visitors to China marvelled at the country's wealth and development. China gave the world many things it now takes for granted, from gunpowder to paper-making and printing. Records made by Chinese astronomers over 2,000 years ago are still referred to today.

It has even been suggested that Italian spaghetti was based on noodles brought back from China by Marco Polo, but this is doubtful. Polo (c1254–c1324) was a Venetian merchant who wrote about his travels in China. Some scholars say he didn't really go there at all, but heard about it from Persian merchants.

Silk and porcelain

Though China is separated from Europe by the huge land mass of central Asia, trade routes between the two flourished as early as Roman times. Silk was exported on camels along the famous 'Silk Route', and also, to some extent, by sea. The Portuguese were the first Europeans to deal directly with China. The Spanish followed, from their new colonies in the Americas, and then the Dutch and the British. From the seventeenth century onwards hundreds of pottery works in south and central China produced huge quantities of porcelain for the export market, which included Latin America as well as Europe and the Middle East.

The neighbouring countries of Korea, Japan and Southeast Asia were strongly influenced by Chinese culture. Japanese art, architecture, religion and writing script all contain many Chinese elements. From the Ming period onwards, many Chinese from the areas around Guangdong and Fujian provinces began to emigrate from their overcrowded countryside to make new homes and start businesses in Southeast Asia.

From the nineteenth century onwards, Chinese immigrants began to arrive in the USA and in Britain. Chinese communities grew up in San Francisco, in Liverpool, and in London's East End. Nowadays most Chinese immigrants in Britain come from Hong Kong.

▲ Papermaking was probably invented in China in the first century AD. Originally, silk and bamboo or wooden strips were used. Then pulp was made from mulberry bark, hemp, worn-out nets and other fibres. By the Tang dynasty, papermaking was a huge industry and an art form.

▼ The earliest surviving example of a Chinese book was found in Central Asia is a Buddhist text known as the Diamond Sutra and is now in the British Museum, London. It is five metres long, and seven woodblocks were used to print it. It was decorated with line drawings.

▲ In China, as in other countries, unwieldy oars were originally used to steer boats. But pottery models of ships excavated from tombs of the 1st century AD prove that rudders fixed to the sterns of boats were in use at this early date.

▲ Chinese potters often adapted their designs for foreign tastes. This early 18th century plate is painted with enamel colours, a style which became popular after the reign of Kang Xi (1661–1722). The picture shows two Scottish soldiers.

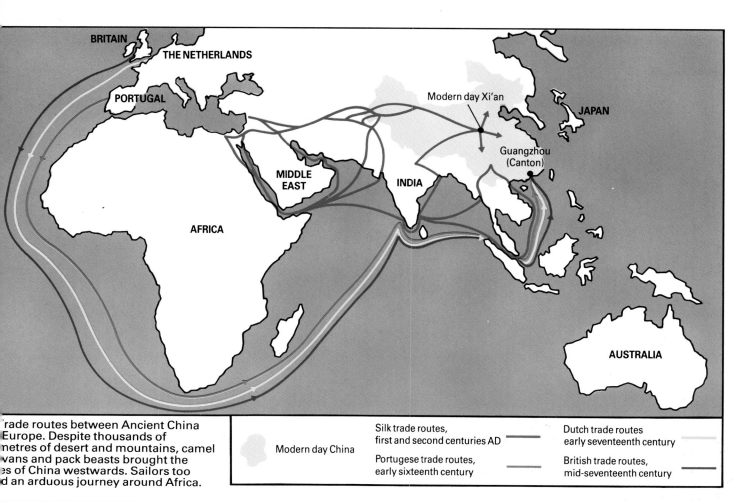

rade routes between Ancient China
Europe. Despite thousands of
netres of desert and mountains, camel
vans and pack beasts brought the
es of China westwards. Sailors too
d an arduous journey around Africa.

Modern day China	Silk trade routes, first and second centuries AD	Dutch trade routes early seventeenth century
	Portugese trade routes, early sixteenth century	British trade routes, mid-seventeenth century

emains of silk have been found in
a dating from 1500 BC, but it was not
the Zhou dynasty (1122 – 221 BC) that
nized silk production ('sericulture')
n. Caterpillars of certain moths are
n mulberry leaves. These produce
ons, from which silk is reeled.

▶ Chinese alchemists had discovered the
secrets of saltpetre (potassium nitrate) as
early as the 8th century AD. They mixed it
with charcoal and sulphur to produce the
first gunpowder. At first this was used for
fireworks, but from the 10th century
onwards it was used in weapons as well.

Late imperial China

Many problems contributed to the downfall of the Qing dynasty. China's population, 300 million in 1787, had risen to 430 million by 1850. Under the long reigns of Kang Xi (1662–1723) and Qian Long (1736–1796), agriculture and technology progressed and the empire expanded its boundaries. Even so, production was unable to keep pace with the growing population.

The problem was made worse by ineffective government and by natural disasters, creating great unhappiness and suffering among the peasants. Popular uprisings, sometimes organized by secret societies, broke out repeatedly in different parts of China from the late eighteenth century onwards. Meanwhile, greedy European traders were waiting to open up the Chinese market. The British were the first to take advantage of China. They had been importing the drug opium into China from India in order to pay for Chinese goods. This was illegal, and in 1839 a mandarin (or official) named Lin Zexu destroyed a consignment of this opium. The British used this as an excuse to start the first 'Opium War'.

The 'Treaty Ports'

British victory led to the first of what are seen by the Chinese as very unfair treaties, which opened up Chinese ports and cities to foreign traders. It was through two of these treaties that Britain gained control of Hong Kong and the New Territories. China was also under pressure from the French in Southeast Asia and from the Japanese in the north east.

Some Chinese officials now thought that the time had come for a reform of the Confucian system of government. Others went further, and suggested a widespread adoption of western ideas and skills, as had happened in Japan. The emperor, Guang Xu, was under the thumb of his father's concubine, the Empress Dowager Ci Xi, and was ineffective as a ruler. People lost faith in this 'Son of Heaven', and felt that foreigners had humiliated China.

These frustrations boiled over in the Boxer Rebellion of 1898. The Manchus staggered on for a few more years, but more and more people hated their weak, corrupt rule.

▲ This French cartoon of 1898 satirizes Britain, Germany, Russia and Japan, who are greedily carving up China between them.

▼ An upper-class opium den in Guangzhou (Canton). The British East India Company exported opium from India to 19th century China. Both rich and poor became addicted to the drug.

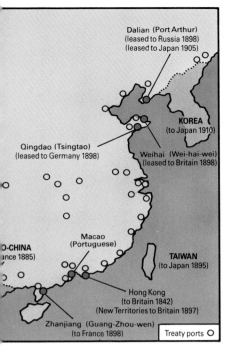

Foreign powers in China in the late 19th [cen]tury.

Imprisoned 'Boxer' rebels. The Boxer [r]ising of 1898 was a northern Chinese [pea]sant movement protesting against [wea]k Qing rule and the foreign powers. [Wit]h approval of Ci Xi, the Boxers (named [fro]m one of their secret societies) [bes]ieged foreign legations, or embassies. [The] foreign powers sent in troops to end [the] siege in 1900.

◀ On 7 January 1841 Chinese war junks were sunk off Guangzhou (Canton) by a fleet which included the steamer *Nemesis*, of the British East India Company. The first Opium War lasted from 1839–42.

▼ The Empress Dowager Ci Xi (1835–1908), the repressive power behind the throne.

Republican China

Sun Yatsen was a doctor from Guangzhou, who was educated in China and Hawaii. He led a revolutionary movement which, after several attempts, finally overthrew the Qing dynasty in 1911. Sun looked to the outside world for ideas. Many of his followers were exiles from China, and anti-Manchu students living abroad.

The warlords

Hopes for the new Republic of China, founded in 1912, were shortlived. Sun was deposed by Yuan Shikai, who in turn lost power in 1916. Warlords controlled various areas of China for the next thirty years. The national government often had no real power, or controlled only a part of the country. For the ordinary people life was much the same as before, if not worse.

A warlord did allow Sun to set up a Nationalist (Guomindang) government in the Guangzhou area in 1921, and Sun tried to bring in some of his reforms. But he died in 1925, and his place was taken by Jiang Jieshi (Chiang K'ai-shek), a less idealistic man whose power lay with the army and the landlord class. Many young

intellectuals, again, often those who had lived abroad, had become disillusioned with the Nationalists' lack of effectiveness and vision. Inspired by the 1917 October Revolution in Russia, they believed that nothing short of a Marxist revolution could help war-torn China and its exhausted people. In 1921 they founded the Chinese Communist Party (CCP).

At first Jiang formed a united front with the Chinese Communist Party, in order to make use of it. But in 1927 betrayed and butchered many Communists in Shanghai, and from then on concentrated on getting rid his Communist rivals, forcing them make the 'Long March'.

In the late 1930s Jiang temporaril joined forces with the CCP, now led by Mao Zedong (Mao Tse-Tung) to fight their common enemy – Japan. After Japan was defeated in 1945, there was bitter civil war between Jiang and the Communists.

▲ The Wuchang Uprising began the process which overthrew Qing rule. In 1911 the New Army mutinied and revolutionaries overthrew a viceroy (imperial governor) in Wuchang. One by one other provinces followed this exampl and established military rule independer of the Qing. Here, viceroys are being escorted away by armed guards.

◄ January 1912: Sun Yatsen (*front row fourth from left*) presides over the founding of the Republic. However conservatives led by Yuan Shikai forced Sun to give up power whilst they secure the abdication of the Qing. The last emperor abdicated in February of that year, and there were limited elections in 1913.

► Key figures of 20th century China line up in front of Guomindang flags. *Left to right*: Liao Zhongkai, Jiang Jieshi, Sun Yatsen, and his wife, Song Qingling (Soc Ching-ling). Song Qingling lived until 1983, a leading communist supporter. He sister married Jiang Jieshi. Liao Zhongk: Sun's closest ally, was assassinated in 1925. His son, Liao Chengzhi, became or of China's leaders after 1949.

...eheaded prisoners are left to rot in the ...et after the Wuchang Uprising, which ...an after a bomb exploded accidentally.

...'uan Shikai, the 'father of the ...lords'. He deposed Sun Yatsen as ...sident in 1912. In 1915 he tried to ...are himself emperor. Civil war broke ...and he was forced to bring back the ...ublic. However it existed in name only, ...China was ruled from 1916–28 by ...less warlords.

...'overty-stricken refugees on the ...kirts of Shanghai. During the ...onalist period (1912–49) both town ...country saw extreme poverty. More ...more people were forced to live in ...sy shelters and beg for scraps. ...usands died.

Socialist revolution

Mao Zedong joined the Chinese Communist Party in 1921 and became its chairman in 1935. He insisted that a rural-based party, fighting a guerrilla war, was most likely to be successful against Jiang's Nationalists with their strongholds in the cities. After the victory over the Nationalists in 1949, the CCP put Marxist theories into practice on a national scale.

Cooperatives and communes
Since eighty percent of China's population lived in the countryside, the CCP's priority on taking power was land reform. Land was redistributed from the landlords to the peasants, and the state took overall control. In the mid-1950s agricultural cooperatives were formed, to be followed in 1958 by 'People's Communes'. These were large, centrally controlled units made up of many villages (known as 'production brigades'), in which the peasants worked for the state rather than on their own land.

This was part of an economic experiment known as the 'Great Leap Forward'. Many people thought that these attempts to reform agriculture and industry were hasty and badly thought out. Unfortunately, the Great Leap Forward was followed by several years of natural disasters, and there was great famine and hardship.

In the early 1960s a power struggle took place within the Chinese government. Some wanted China to remain rigidly socialist, with the state in complete control. Others wanted more economic freedom. Mao was afraid that economic freedom would lead to the re-emergence of the middle classes and capitalists.

The 'Cultural Revolution'
In 1966 Mao decided to start a 'Cultural Revolution', to change people's ideas. He encouraged students to attack people taking what was known as the 'capitalist road'. These were usually officials, intellectuals and middle-class people. Mao's wife, Jiang Qing, took control of the country's new anti-western cultural programme. Chaos spread and universities, schools and factories closed down. The country came to a virtual standstill. In 1976, Zhou Enlai, China's popular premier, who had deftly managed to stay in power throughout the ten years of the Cultural Revolution, died of cancer. There were demonstrations in Beijing openly deploring the situation in China and mourning Zhou.

When Mao Zedong died later that year, the group of people who had been most influential in the 'Cultural Revolution' tried to take complete control. They were nicknamed the 'Gang of Four', and included Jiang Qing. But they were caught and imprisoned. The Cultural Revolution was finally over.

▼ The Long March lasted from 1934–36. The CCP, after repeated attacks from the Guomindang, moved their base to the Jingganshan area of Jiangxi Province. Here they set up a communist system, or 'soviet', based on land reform. They recruited peasants to their cause, and decided to rely on guerilla warfare, avoiding the cities. Between 1930 and 1934 Jiang Jieshi tried to dislodge them.

Finally the CCP broke through Jiang's blockade. Men, women, children, soldiers and local peasants set off on the Long March. They passed through Guizhou and Yunnan, crossed the wild Upper Yangzi, skirted Tibet and marched through Gansu before reaching Yan'an. All along the route they were attacked, and suffered dreadfully from cold and hunger.

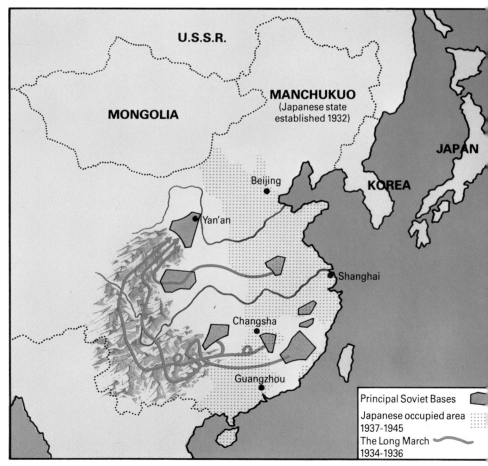

Principal Soviet Bases

Japanese occupied area 1937-1945

The Long March 1934-1936

▲ In November 1943 Jiang Jieshi and his wife met US President Roosevelt and British Prime Minister Churchill in Cairo. They declared that Manchuria and Taiwan would become part of China again, whilst Korea would become independent.

▼ The turbulent years of the 'Cultural Revolution'. These local government offices in Beijing have been closed by Red Guards, some of whom have travelled hundreds of kilometres to find out what is going on.

Mao Zedong, chairman of the CCP, orts to the Lu Xun Arts Institute in an, 1938. After the Long March, an became the base area for the munists. Land reforms were carried n the area and sympathisers flocked to communist cause from all over China.

Mao Zedong led China from 1949 to 6. His influence in China was rmous, and people would study not Marxism-Leninism, but also his many ngs, known as the 'Thoughts of Mao ong'. Poet, philosopher and soldier, was hero-worshipped in his day. e portraits and statues of him were everywhere.

China and the world today

In 1949, as the CCP's People's Liberation Army was advancing, Jiang Jieshi fled mainland China. He and his Nationalists went to Taiwan, and he became head of a virtually one-party state, the Republic of China. His son took control of Taiwan after Jiang's death.

However the rulers on the mainland (which became known as the *People's* Republic of China) believe that Taiwan, like Hong Kong, is a part of their country which will one day be returned to them. Originally Taiwan was heavily backed by the USA. But in 1972 US President Richard Nixon and Henry Kissinger resumed relations with the People's Republic, and the USA had to deal with both Chinas. Strong links between the USA and the mainland government were not really forged until the late 1970s.

Deng Xiaoping

China's new outward-looking attitude was encouraged by Deng Xiaoping. This wily politican had twice been banished from power when he returned to lead China in the late 1970s. His visit to the USA in 1979 marked a new era in China's relations with the western world. Deng was in charge of the talks with Britain which agreed that, with certain conditions, China should take control of the colony of Hong Kong when the lease on the New Territories ran out in 1997.

With Premier Zhao Ziyang and Hu Yaobang (General Secretary of the CCP) Deng encouraged foreign investment in China and stressed the development of light industry. One of Deng's biggest changes was to get rid of the commune system and allow the peasants more responsibility for their own land.

The future of socialism

In earlier years Deng had once said of socialism, 'who cares whether a cat is black or white, so long as it catches mice'. This view was certainly not shared by those in control during the 'Cultural Revolution'. To them it was better to be 'red' (a good socialist) than 'expert' (someone who puts their profession before their politics). Deng however was able to foresee a China in the early twenty-first century as

▲ In 1971 China, now a nuclear power, was admitted to the United Nations Organization (UNO). In the following ye[ar] US President Nixon visited China and m[et] Mao Zedong (*above*) and Zhou Enlai. Th[e] USA agreed to 'normalize' relations.

◄ A Chinese prisoner captured by the Vietnamese during the war of 1979. Vietnam, united under communist rule since its defeat of the USA-backed south[,] was now too friendly with the USSR for China's liking. Troops from the two land[s] clashed along the border.

'one country with two systems': socialist China side-by-side with capitalist Hong Kong.

Such 'pro-capitalist' tendencies were frowned upon by the Soviet Union. China had been at odds with its socialist neighbour since 1960, when Soviet advisers were expelled from China and their contracts torn up, because of political and economic disagreements.

In the 1980s however, relations have improved. China and the USSR are both influential in Third World politics, and this has sometimes led to a clash of interests – in Vietnam, for example.

SONY

希望通过这些产品在各方面向中国朋友们提供方便。 **Only Sony has it all.**

China and Britain came to an ~~agree~~ment over Hong Kong in 1984. ~~Briti~~sh Prime Minister Thatcher and ~~Forei~~gn Secretary Howe are seen here ~~celeb~~rating in the Great Hall of the People, ~~Bei~~jing. Their host is Li Xiannian, the ~~Presi~~dent of China.

▲ Advertisement hoardings replace political posters outside Beijing's Peking Hotel. In the background is Wang Fu Jing, the city's main shopping street. People now want the 'Four Goods': a washing machine, a fridge, a television and a radio-cassette player.

▼ Deng Xiaoping, then vice-premier of China, visits a rodeo and barbecue in Houston, Texas. Deng's visit in 1979 was the first by a senior Chinese politican and delegation. Chinese television viewers back home were amazed by the prosperity of the United States.

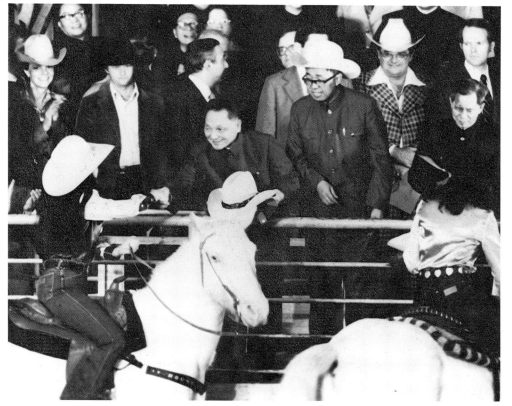

Industry and commerce

For centuries, the Chinese economy was based on agriculture and crafts. Although China had made many important inventions, it was in Europe that great advances were made in technology and engineering. This 'Industrial Revolution' of the eighteenth and nineteenth centuries did not reach China until the end of the last century. Even then, such industries as developed were mostly confined to the western-controlled 'Treaty Ports'. They included textiles, tobacco, food, printing, banking and wholesale trade.

The 1920s, 30s and 40s were unsettled years and industry stagnated. When the communists came to power, many 'compradors' (foreign-influenced traders) fled to Hong Kong. But others remained and were used from 1950–56 in 'joint enterprises'. The aim of these was to develop basic industries in China. The Soviet Union provided equipment and assistance, and at first China followed the Soviet example of concentrating upon heavy industry rather than agriculture.

But Mao Zedong began to have doubts about this policy, and in 1958 the CCP called for a 'Great Leap forward'. Agriculture and rural industries were to be developed alongside heavy industry. Mao's policy was not a success, and when the Soviet Union withdrew in 1960, it only made matters worse. In the early 1960s Mao's opponents argued that expert scientists and industrialists rather than politicians should control factories, and that industry should offer workers more rewards. These ideas were totally rejected during the 'Cultural Revolution', but found favour with the Chinese leadership after Mao's death in 1976.

Opening the door

China's overall leader in the following years was Deng Xiaoping. He welcomed foreign trade and investment and from 1977 onwards called for 'the four modernizations' in agriculture, industry, science and technology, and defence. 'Special Economic Zones' such as Shenzhen (between Guangzhou and Hong Kong) were set up in order to encourage foreign involvement. Huge orders for advanced technology were placed abroad. However inexperience meant that mistakes were made.

In the mid-1980s Deng's 'Open Door' policies were still being followed. He felt his agricultural reforms had been successful, and that industry and commerce should be more competitive. He encouraged foreign firms to invest in China and train Chinese workers in technological skills. In addition to this 'transfer of technology' Deng encouraged the appointment of new, younger managers.

Deng's critics felt that these were not proper policies for a socialist state. They wanted to see more state planning and felt that the recent changes had had a corrupting influence. They even doubted the

success of the agricultural reforms.

Control of the economy was tightened up a little, but the directio[n] remained the same. The future of China's industry, and of its trade w[ith] the outside world, remains a matter for debate.

◄ A Japanese buyer negotiates the sal[e] of handmade Chinese tablecloths in Dalian, an important industrial and commercial centre in the northeast. In th[e] mid-1980s some anti-Japanese feeling resurfaced in China. People protested th[at] Japanese businessmen had sold China second-rate goods.

A new look for the Chinese economy: [Sha]ntou (Swatow) Special Economic Zone [nea]r Guangzhou. These women are [wor]king in a factory owned by a Hong [Kon]g-based company. Wages in such [fact]ories are often higher than in ordinary [Chi]nese ones. Both carpets and blankets [are] made here, and exported to Japan and [the] USA.

▲ A country market in Sichuan province. Stall holders are supposed to pay a tax to the local government, but are otherwise free to sell what they wish and charge whatever price they want. Items for sale include cheap clothes and shoes.

▲ The Gezhouba scheme on the Yangzi Jiang. This huge complex dams the river just below the famous Yangzi Gorges in Sichuan province. It controls floods and offers improved navigation and irrigation facilities. It also generates power, and China's hydroelectric potential is increasingly important.

▲ Foreign cooperation: British Petroleum (BP) carrying out exploratory drilling in the South China Sea. Operation of the semi-submersible rig is contracted out to a Chinese corporation. There are oilfields in northeast China (the most famous of which is Daqing) in the mouth of the Huang He, as well as in Qinghai and Hubei.

Beijing: the capital of China

Beijing, or Peking, is in the north of China. To the north and west are mountains, whilst to the south and east lies the North China Plain. Beijing occupies a strategic position and was capital of China as early as the Liao, Jin and Yuan dynasties.

Even so, Beijing is still smaller than Shanghai, which has a population of nearly 12 million. People from Shanghai, which has a lot of grand buildings, dating from its days as a Treaty Port, used to call Beijing the 'big village'. Today Beijing is beginning to take on the appearance of a major international capital and is home to over 9 million people.

Beijing has been the centre of government and communications since 1949. New buildings were constructed at that time in the architectural style of the Soviet Union, especially around Tian An Men Square and along Chang An Jie, the central boulevard that cuts across Beijing. The new building and road works meant the destruction of ancient lanes and walled compounds, and of the spectacular city walls. Some of today's planners try to make sure that new buildings do not disturb the older parts of the city.

Temples and Palaces

Beijing has many historical sites, such as the Temple of Heaven, and the Summer Palace, the summer retreat of the Empress Dowager Ci Xi. In the countryside to the north of the capital are the Ming Tombs and the Great Wall. The Forbidden City (or Imperial Palace) takes up a large area in the centre of Beijing, and is made up of nearly ten thousand rooms: the largest collection of ancient buildings in the world. It was built in the fifteenth century, and was the home of the imperial court during periods when Beijing was the capital.

The centre of government

Beijing is now the home of China's socialist government, which believes that the workers form the most important class, and that they exerc power through the Chinese Communist Party. Though China is governed by the CCP, people do not call themselves 'communists'. They say they are 'socialists', by which the mean people who are trying to become communists and at the same time bring about a communist societ There are between 30 and 40 million CCP members, about 4 per cent of t total population. China is really a one-party state, although other part and groups, including overseas Chinese, are represented in the Chinese People's Political Consultative Conference. There are no general elections, but since the death of Mao there have been some local elections. Other recent change include reform of the legal system an a reduction in the size of the People' Liberation Army from 4 to 3 million soldiers. The government breaks down into two groups, as shown in the diagram on the left: the CCP and the administration.

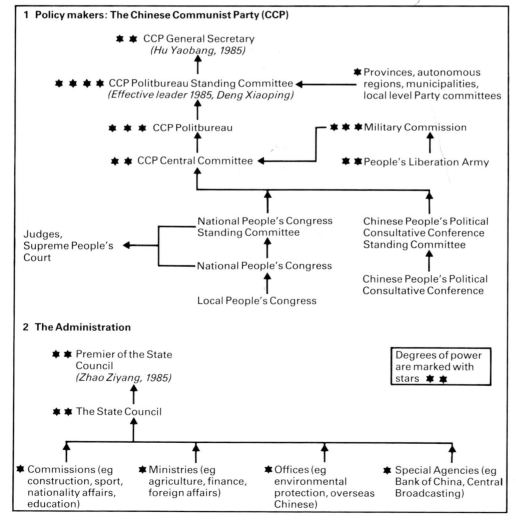

1 Policy makers: The Chinese Communist Party (CCP)

★ ★ CCP General Secretary *(Hu Yaobang, 1985)*

★ ★ ★ ★ CCP Politbureau Standing Committee ← ★ Provinces, autonomous regions, municipalities, local level Party committees *(Effective leader 1985, Deng Xiaoping)*

★ ★ ★ CCP Politbureau ← ★ ★ ★ Military Commission

★ ★ CCP Central Committee ← ★ ★ People's Liberation Army

Judges, Supreme People's Court ← National People's Congress Standing Committee

National People's Congress — Chinese People's Political Consultative Conference Standing Committee

Local People's Congress — Chinese People's Political Consultative Conference

2 The Administration

★ ★ Premier of the State Council *(Zhao Ziyang, 1985)*

★ ★ The State Council

Degrees of power are marked with stars ★ ★

★ Commissions (eg construction, sport, nationality affairs, education)

★ Ministries (eg agriculture, finance, foreign affairs)

★ Offices (eg environmental protection, overseas Chinese)

★ Special Agencies (eg Bank of China, Central Broadcasting)

▲ Young Pioneers (China's equivalent of scouts and guides) flying kites. Chang An Jie boulevard crosses the Square of Heavenly Peace, where rallies and parades are held. The Gate of Heavenly Peace (Tian An Men), entrance to the Forbidden City, is in the background.

► A lane (*hutong*) in the older part of Beijing. This part of the city has many trees, and people grow canopies of climbing plants to act as cool porches in the summer. On hot summer evenings people like to cook and eat in the inner courtyards or on the pavements.

▼ The eastern part of Beijing, looking towards the Western Hills. Many new blocks of flats are being built to meet the desperate housing shortage. Difficulty in supply of water and electricity sometimes means that the new buildings stand empty.

Tourists and day-trippers recording r visit to the Temple of Heaven. Built ng the Ming dynasty, the temple bolized heaven and earth. This was re the emperor acted out important ls. He would pray for good harvests guidance in government matters.

Town and country

Life in a Chinese city is very different from that in the countryside. Mao Zedong recognized early in his career that the relationship between town and country was one of China's major problems, and this is still true today. Since 1949, great improvements have been made in the general quality of life in rural China. Even so, a peasant's day is usually more gruelling and monotonous than that of a city-dweller.

In northern China peasants grow wheat and millet. From spring to autumn they work all day, ploughing, sowing, irrigating, weeding and harvesting. Winter is spent repairing tools and machinery, building houses, or taking part in communal projects like land reclamation.

In the south, some green crops can be grown in the early spring, before the rice is planted in the paddy fields. Hard work is therefore called for all year round, and it is here that the need for many helpers, especially boys, is greatest.

Facilities such as clinics, schools and small shops are largely operated by local government, at a village or district level. In recent years a few of these have become privately owned. Peasants may sell their produce to government-run stores or directly to the public in 'free markets'. These are cheaper and very popular with shoppers.

In the towns, facilities such as children's nurseries and part-time workshops are taken care of by one's workplace 'unit' or by a neighbourhood committee. The unit, or local government, also allocates cheap rented accommodation.

Town dwellers enjoy cinemas, theatre, restaurants, youth 'palaces' and libraries. But cities have disadvantages too, such as overcrowding. Families may live in one or two rooms, with shared kitchens and lavatories and communal baths. There is often a lack of town planning, and services can be haphazard. Industrial and domestic fuel pollution can pose severe problems.

Nevertheless, towns and cities are attractive to country people, who yearn for city life and think they can make more money there. The government has to do its best to sto people moving in from the country and swelling the city population.

Rural responsibility

In recent years, the Chinese government completely reorganized the rural economy. The 'People's Communes' introduced by Mao wer replaced by the 'Responsibility System'. Peasant farmers now took out contracts with the state to grow what they wanted in land allocated their family. An annual tax was paic to the state, sometimes in the form c crops specified by the government. I family grew more than it needed, the extra produce could be sold. These reforms allowed peasants to increas their income. It was hoped that mor mechanized farming would release more people to work in rural industries.

In towns, light industry has been concentrated upon rather than the traditional heavy industries such as engineering. It is cheaper to set up a to run, supplies the growing consun market, and uses more workers. Thi last point has been very important, a a high birth rate in the 1950s and 6(led to growing urban unemploymen

At the heart of these recent reforn are age-old preoccupations. China aims at self-sufficiency, and does no wish to import grain. The peasant farmer holds the key to the survival the town dweller, and of the nation a whole.

▲ A peasant farmer's family house in Fengyang county, Anhui province. It was in this county that the 'Responsibility System' was first tried out. The tiled roof in the background shows that the farmer is comparatively well-off: poorer people use thatch. Feeding the pigs and tending the crops is hard and often cold work. In winter suits of padded cotton are worn.

▶ A 'free market' in Harbin, a large city in northeast China. Traders are selling ice lollies and fruit squash. The lollies, in the white box, are kept cool in padded compartments. The fruit squash is dispensed from a modern, imported machine, not seen until recently in China. Small street stalls like these are very common in the towns.

oeing a sweet potato field in central
a. Although tractors are becoming
common, a lot of work is still done
and, with all the family joining in. In
near towns women often do the
work while the men look for jobs in
stry. Irrigation is a problem in this part
ina. Where there is enough water,
at, millet and soya beans are grown.

▲ Datong is a northern town famous for
coalmining. Its houses are arranged in
compounds around a central courtyard.
Several families live in each compound,
and often cook out of doors, even in
winter. In the picture you can see New
Year 'couplets' around the door, chili
peppers hanging to dry, and a chicken
shed.

▼ Peasant farmers from Anhui province
get down to one of the autumn's chores,
sifting through the seeds of winter wheat.
They are checking virtually every grain for
signs of mould or disease. These farmers
are quite well off, but some areas of Anhui
are arid and suitable only for growing
sweet potatoes, a crop introduced from
the Americas in the 16th century.

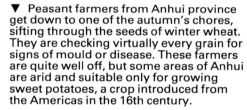

Population and health

In 1982 a census was taken in China. It showed a population of over 1,008 million people, nearly a quarter of all mankind. The population had almost doubled since 1949. One reason for this was the great improvement in living conditions and health care. In 1949 life expectancy was only 35 years, but by 1980 it was 69 years. Another reason however was the lack of an effective birth control policy before 1971. Indeed, in the 1950s China had followed the Soviet Union's example and actually encouraged population growth.

People and planning
After 1971 family planning was emphasized, allied with improved social welfare. The birth rate would have to be reduced by a quarter. Since half the population was under twenty-one, it looked like being a very difficult undertaking.

A large campaign to promote family planning was set in motion in 1981. Late marriage and late childbirth were encouraged as before, but now the requirement was that each family should have only one child, except in the thinly-populated ethnic minority areas. This was brought about by strong social and official pressure. Contraception supplies were publicized, and facilities for abortion made more available.

Parents who had only one child were now rewarded. It was to be easier for them to enrol their child in a nursery, school, or factory, and easier to obtain medical treatment and certain goods, especially foodstuffs. Single-child families were the first to receive housing plots in the countryside or rooms and flats in towns. In some workplace units cash benefits were offered as well, which had to be repaid if a second was born.

Family traditions
It is hard to change traditional views overnight. It is still considered unnatural to want only one child in China. Boys are preferred because people believe that they are stronger and can work harder on the land. Girls, when they marry, go to live with their husband's family. Parents worry about who will look after them in their old age, and who will carry on the family name. Very occasionally feelings have been so strong that baby girls have been killed at birth.

The new ideas are not enforced rigidly, and most people understand that overpopulation is an urgent problem. Even so, there is some personal resentment, and misgiving. People are also concerned that an only child will be spoilt and over-protected, and so grow up to be selfish.

Welfare and medicine
Providing for the elderly is one way in which the government can help allay fears for the future. The state is supposed to provide 'Five Guarantees' for old people who have no family to look after them. These are: food, clothing, housing, medical care and burial expenses. There are still some who are not provided for, however, and many poor families find it difficult to care for elderly relations.

State employees and workers have free medical care and medicine, and can also get sick pay, maternity pay and pensions. Peasants don't get these benefits and have to pay money for medical care into a central fund at local government level. They may also have to pay for each visit to a clinic or hospital.

▲ A man of the Dai ethnic group chops fresh herbs at a clinic attached to a hospital in southern China. The herbs will probably be dried and stored in wooden drawers. When a prescription is called for, they will be weighed out and mixed. They are then boiled, and the liquid drunk.

Before 1949 disease was rife in China. Today many of the problems have been brought under control. Health education at a local level has taught people the benefits of hygiene and preventive medicine. In the countryside the word is often spread by healthcare workers who can provide first aid and simple medical treatment. In the Cultural Revolution period they were known as 'barefoot doctors' because they worked in the fields as well.

Traditional Chinese medicine makes use of herbs and acupuncture, a treatment that involves sticking needles into areas of the skin. Both are still used, especially for mild or long-term illnesses, and have in recent years become popular outside China. Modern medical methods developed in the west are used more for acute infectious illnesses, or in surgery.

...is poster encourages people to have ...child families, and emphasizes that ...ts should welcome girl children as ... as boys.

...poor woman and child beg for relief ...g the Communists' struggle to take ...g. She sits in front of a Moslem ...urant in the Tian Qiao amusement ... Living conditions improved ...derably in the years after 1949.

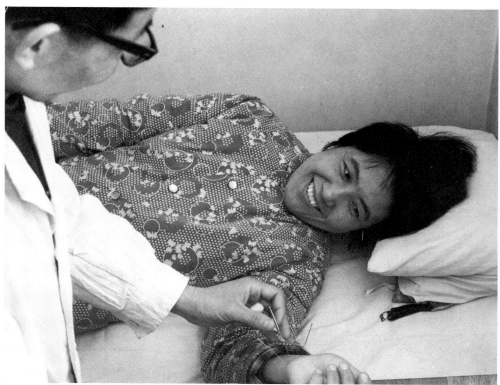

▼ A dentist and patient in a village clinic near Guangzhou. Facilities for doctors and dentists are still often rather basic, but are much better than they were. There are check-ups at school, but most people wait until they have bad toothache before paying a visit to the dental clinic. Cosmetic dentistry is very rare.

▲ A patient is treated for a nervous condition by acupuncture. The treatment, which was invented in ancient China, involves sticking very sharp, fine, sterilized needles into the body. They are rotated gently by hand, or sometimes made to vibrate electrically. The needles relieve symptoms in other parts of the body.

Family life

The family is very important in China. Confucius taught that duty and obedience are important within the family, and some of these ideas still persist in China today.

A child's duty

Children in China are expected to feel (and often do feel) that they owe their parents a great deal for bringing them up and for supporting them in their early years. So when their parents are ill or elderly, they feel they should look after them and give way to their wishes, even if only for the sake of appearances.

Marriage and raising children

A parent tends to feel that a child should be under firm control until he or she is well established in a job and ready to marry, though early marriages (before the mid-twenties) are discouraged. Parents, colleagues, friends, and even marriage bureaux and paid go-betweens often help to match suitable marriage partners. Single people vetted in this way usually feel grateful and reassured. However, if the couple who have been introduced don't hit it off, they are quite free to go their separate ways.

Divorce is still very much a last resort in China, with strong social and official pressure to keep a marriage going. Problems in marriages may occur because of cramped living conditions or shortage of money. The

▼ A special banquet for a family in Chengdu, capital of Sichuan province. This is a rich agricultural area, and there is plenty of food: beancurd in spicy mince, fish, pork, peppers, chili and beans are being served. Sichuan cooking is very hot and spicy.

▲ The home of a laboratory technicia Harbin. The family of four live in a thre room flat with its own kitchen – luxuric accommodation by Chinese standards Both adults work for a total income of about £50 per month. Rent and service cost £2.50 a month.

uilding traditional houses in the
ills of the Tian Shan (Heavenly
ntains) in Xinjiang. Logs are used to
e walls of mud, and the roof will
ably be thatched. The builders are
Chinese, but they are living in the
eland of the Kazakh people.

simple lunch at home for a southern
ese family. Rice is eaten in large
ntities, and there are three cooked
es. A bottle of soy sauce adds flavour.
hern Chinese have a greater choice of
tables than their northern
nbours.

his grandmother is looking after her
ddaughter whose parents are out at
, perhaps in the fields. Until recent
children's clothes were much
iter than adults', but nowadays many
s buy the most stylish they can afford.
r people still prefer more traditional
s.

he dogkennel-like hut in the
round would have been home to two
ies before 1949. It has been kept to
nd people of the bad old days.

'in-laws' often live with the family,
and this too can be a cause of stress.

Retired grandparents are usually
very keen to look after children of pre-
school age, even if this means a child
living with them and not with the
parents. This can lead to problems
when the child has to return home in
later years, but it does mean that both
parents can work full-time.

Many young children in cities spend
all day in nurseries and only see their
parents, who both work, at night.
Some even spend all week in a nursery
and only see their parents on Sundays.

Eating and drinking
Although many Chinese men cook
extremely well and may also help with
the housework, it is still usually the
woman who tackles the household
chores and cooks the main meal of the
day. This is often lunch. A family's
social life centres around food. In
towns, meat, if any, and vegetables
are bought fresh each day, as
refrigerators are still a luxury in
China. There are often long queues in
the shops and markets.

Vegetables form the bulk of the
food. Meat and eggs are expensive
and are used sparingly. Fish is very

popular. The style of cooking varies a
great deal from one region to another,
but Chinese cuisine is generally
recognized as one of the world's best.

Even in poor areas, the family sits
down to several dishes of food at a
time. Everyone takes what they want
from each dish, bit by bit, with their
chopsticks. They each have a bowl of
rice, noodles or steamed buns as the
basis of the meal. Soup is served last,
to fill any gaps. Children are often not
allowed soup, as it is supposed to
dilute the digestive juices.

Much of the conversation at the
table and afterwards will be about
food. People are sometimes quite
critical. At festivals and weddings
huge quantities of food are prepared
by the whole family, often with the
help of neighbours and friends.

Processed foods such as sweets and
soft drinks are becoming popular in
China, as are expensive imported
cigarettes. There is little awareness of
the health risks involved, and smoking
is very fashionable when business
people or officials have meetings and
entertain. There are few bars in
China. People drink alcohol at home
with meals or in restaurants, on
special occasions.

33

Education and young people

Children in China start primary school at the age of seven. Primary schooling is not available everywhere in China and the government is trying to provide more facilities for the countryside, such as mobile schools for remote areas.

Children study subjects similar to those in Britain or elsewhere, but the Confucian tradition of learning still lingers on in some aspects of education. Chinese children spend a lot of time learning things by heart or memorizing things they do not fully understand.

It is up to the teacher to provide information, make the children learn it, and check that they have done so. Until the late 1970s political education was stressed rather than academic values, but today the reverse is true. Much of the timetable is taken up by study of the Chinese language, which is a very long process. This is perhaps one reason why, according to some people, Chinese children are given less time to develop their initiative and independence.

Secondary school and college

At the age of thirteen, most children in large and medium-sized cities go to junior 'middle' school, where they spend three years. In the countryside, children who don't continue their education go out to work in the fields. Even those who do go to school frequently help out in home-based work after school to boost the family income.

At sixteen, after leaving a school in a town, young people might go to a factory for a three-year apprenticeship, or study at a technical college. Jobs are allocated by the state in China, but some become unemployed.

There are 145 million children in primary schools in China, and some 55 million in junior and senior 'middle' schools. Only just over a million go on to receive higher education, after very stiff entrance exams. Of these, a tiny minority try another exam which allows them to study abroad on a government grant.

New fashions

Since Mao Zedong's death in 1976, many young people have been keen to follow overseas fashions in music,

dress and behaviour. This is easier for them to do if they live in the cities. Some have also looked to western ideas about individual rights and democracy in their search for political reform. When these ideas have been expressed in underground magazines and meetings they have sometimes been met with strong measures from the government.

During the Cultural Revolution (1966–76) many 'educated young people', as they were known, were encouraged to move to the countryside to help the peasants. Some settled down and married in the area to which they were sent. Others have tried in recent years to return to their homes, which are often in overcrowded cities like Beijing and Shanghai. They are often unable to find work or permanent places to live. This has resulted in a rash of small private enterprises such as cafés or market stalls, and also, unfortunately, in a rising crime rate.

During the 1980s the Chinese government became increasingly aware that it should provide strong leadership and incentives for its large number of young people, and tried to change the situation.

▲ A pupil learns to write the many Chinese characters with a brush. This particular style of writing is known as *dakai*. It is important to hold the brush in the correct way. A stick of dried ink is rubbed with water on to an ink-stone. The brush is dipped in repeatedly as the characters are written. A strict order of brush strokes has to be followed.

▲ Until the late 19th century, the main aim of Chinese education was to study works associated with the philosopher Confucius (Kong Fu Zi), who lived from 551–479 BC. They are known as the 'Confucian Classics', but it is thought th in reality only one work is by Confucius himself, the *Analects*. This is made up o fragments of dialogue.

▲ In China, physical education is thought to be every bit as important as classroom study. There are specialist schools and colleges for pupils who show a talent for sports.

◄ First form pupils take part in a maths competition. New teaching methods are being tried out at this experimental primary school in Liaoning province. Teaching standards are usually high.

▼ The library at Fudan University, Shanghai. There is fierce competition for all further education. Students must work hard and live in crowded dormitories.

Arts and literature

Before the twentieth century, ordinary people in China rarely learned to read and write. Books were written in classical Chinese, a form of the language that was about as different from everyday speech as is Anglo-Saxon from modern English.

Writing for a new China

In the early twentieth century there were calls for this situation to be changed. Radical anti-foreign demonstrations broke out on May 4 1919 as students called for a new literature, written in the style of the modern spoken language.

One of the first writers to use such a style was Lu Xun, China's most famous modern author. He expressed the problems facing people who were still rooted in Chinese traditions, but who wanted to reach forward to new ideas and practices.

After 1949, writers were encouraged to write optimistic, reassuring works for the masses. The government tended to clamp down on any books which they felt were too outspoken, cynical or individualistic. During the Cultural Revolution (1966–76) Jiang Qing took control of arts policy in China. Many writers, artists and musicians were persecuted by the authorities.

Arts and crafts today

After the downfall of the 'Gang of Four' in 1976, Chinese cultural life began to change again. Traditional Chinese operas reappeared, with their mixture of highly stylized singing, drama, acrobatics and martial arts.

Traditional Chinese musicians played folk tunes and imperial court music again, and western-style orchestras went back to playing works by European composers. Foreign pop song tapes began to appear on the black market, while even the official market sold taped imitations of western songs. The film industry flourished. Many Chinese films seem sentimental and old-fashioned to Europeans, but they are well-received and much discussed in China.

Many Chinese artists and craft workers practise skills which have often remained unchanged for centuries. There are several museums

▲ Traditional Beijing Opera being performed in the theatre at Taiyuan, capital of Shanxi province. Heroes have their faces painted in simple colours, whilst villains and rough characters paint their faces with complicated designs. Costumes are very ornate. Mime is used to great effect.

▼ Talented pupils study traditional musical instruments at a middle school Zhengzhou. The *yang qin* or Chinese dulcimer has strings which are hit with sticks. The *er hu* is a kind of violin. It has two strings and the bow is played betwe them. Many overseas Chinese have thei own orchestras which perform regularl

galleries in Britain and Europe
ere you can see fine examples of
inese painting, pottery, sculpture,
er, lacquerware and furniture.
ere is a strong tradition of folk art
China, expressed in papercuts, New
ar pictures and village handicrafts.
u can often buy examples of these
tside China. Chinese political art,
h as the propaganda posters which
came famous in the 1960s, has
gely been replaced by commercial
vertising.

Lu Xun (1881–1936) photographed in
anghai in 1933. China's leading modern
thor founded the Literary Association,
ter the patriotic demonstrations of 1919,
d the League of Left-Wing Writers in
30. He thought that literature should
flect social life and be something more
an just a pleasant pastime.

▼ Painting according to tradition. The
'flower and bird' style originated in the
Tang dynasty and was influenced by
Buddhist art. Painting and the brush-
writing of characters are closely related in
Chinese art. In this small studio paintings
in the ancient style are being produced for
sale.

▲ Near Luoyang, in Henan province, are
the famous Buddhist carvings of Long
Men. Thousands of niches and statues
were carved out of the limestone cliffs in
the 5th century AD. They show the Indian
influence on art and religion during this
period. In the foreground are foreign
students on a Spring Festival outing.

▼ This oil-painting is a self-portrait by
Zhu Jingshi, a member of the 'Star' group
of Chinese artists. This unofficial group
appeared in Beijing in the late 1970s.
Their work shocked many people.

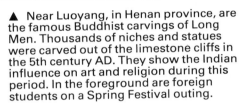

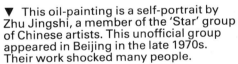

Leisure and sport

Leisure is enjoyed in China, but people do not necessarily think of it as their right, as tends to happen in more industrialized countries. Nowadays, work is becoming more mechanized and political activities take up less time than they used to. This means that people, particularly in the towns, are today able to make use of more free time.

In the countryside peasants often spend their evenings making small items for sale, if they work in the fields during the day, or tending their crops if they work in industrial cooperatives. They also enjoy eating, visiting each other and watching television or films in a communal hall.

Some richer peasants now have their own televisions. Town dwellers too watch a lot of television, as many have their own sets, or watch with neighbours.

People of all ages in the towns and cities enjoy 'do-it-yourself' activities: making furniture, improving their homes, mending bicycles, making clothes, and growing indoor plants. Young people like to learn foreign languages, especially English, from the radio or television.

There is usually little space or privacy in their homes, so at weekends or in the evenings they often meet in parks or just stroll around the streets. Dancing is becoming very popular. It is mostly in the ballroom style, but disco-dancing is allowed within certain limits.

Holiday outings

Sometimes people go on day trips to historic sites or to the seaside, if they can afford it. National festivals are holidays for all, and four days holiday is taken at the Chinese New Year (the Spring Festival). People who live away from home are given one month's annual leave to visit their families: this is often at Spring Festival and is a favourite time for weddings and betrothals. Some 'model' workers (people who have done especially well at their jobs) may qualify for a week or two's holiday at a health centre or seaside resort.

Elderly people in China take an active part in family and community life. In the early mornings they may exercise in parks or other open space or take pet songbirds in cages for a stroll. During the day they may look after the grandchildren, or sit in tea houses for hours on end and listen to traditional story tellers.

Public parks are often full of activity, especially in the early mornings and at weekends. People of all ages practise singing, musical instruments, and foreign languages.

Olympic challengers

Since the early 1950s, sport has been an important part of the school timetable. There are good facilities for games in town schools, and access to swimming pools. The most popular sports are table-tennis, badminton, basketball and athletics. Children and adults do exercises to broadcast radio music twice a day, and martial arts, taught at school, keep people fit.

Since 1976 China has trained football teams which play at international level, and has competed successfully all over the world in table tennis, athletics, weight-lifting, swimming and gymnastic competitions. In 1984 in Los Angeles, USA, China took part in the Olympic Games for the first time.

▲ A panda called Qingqing draws the crowds in Fuzhou Zoo. Pandas live in the wilder parts of Sichuan province and eat bamboo. A shortage of this shrub has led to fears of the panda dying out. It is now officially protected.

► Retired men playing cards in a Beijing street. Shaven heads are a common fashion, especially for men and small children. Their wives will be at home cooking, looking after grandchildren, or helping to run a local committee.

▲ Tian An Men Square in Beijing is the scene of early morning martial arts practice. This activity is called *jianwu*, and makes use of swordplay. Steel swords may be used by those who can afford them, but wood or plastic ones are good enough for practice. Martial arts (known as *Wu shu*) are very popular. Some have become fashionable in the west. *Tai ji quan* is Chinese shadow boxing, a slow rhythmic exercise popular in China amongst old people. *Gong fu* (Kung Fu), with its high jumps and kicks, is performed by young people.

 crowded swimming pool in Beijing. nming pools are normally mixed, but do not think it right to wear bikinis. re you can use a pool you have to a blood test to prove that you are thy. Swimming is popular as a leisure ity and sport.

▶ The Beijing basketball team, in 1983 stars of the national sports meeting, held in the capital. The national men's team member Guo Yonglin (*first left*) helped China reach the 1984 Olympic Games in Los Angeles, the first time the People's Republic had competed.

Transport and tourism

In imperial China communications were very poor. Transport relied on draught animals and manpower. 'Coolies' carried heavy loads on their backs, or pulled two-wheeled wooden carts. Boats transported freight along rivers and canals. Most traffic was local, between market towns and the surrounding countryside. Road, ferries and fords were at the mercy of rains and floods.

The foreign powers who traded in China in the nineteenth century brought their own technology. The British built China's first railway in 1876. A foreign-built railway network grew up, but it was badly damaged during the war years of the 1930s and 40s. It was a priority for improvement in 1949.

Today the rail system is used to capacity, although (as in many Asian countries) there are still problems in moving large quantities of goods over long distances. When travelling by train you often have to queue several times, especially if you want a sleeper berth as well as a ticket. Steam trains are still widely used in China, and during the peak holiday period of the Spring Festival goods trains are sometimes used to transport passengers.

The most common vehicle in modern China is the bicycle. There are still very few private cars, and motorways have only just begun to appear in China. Bridge-building, road-metalling and repairs have all improved greatly since 1949. Transport remains a problem in remote areas such as Tibet and Xinjiang.

Canals are still used to carry a great deal of freight, including stretches of the famous Grand Canal which in imperial times linked Beijing with Hangzhou, south of the Yangzi Jiang. A quarter of the Chinese river network is navigable.

There are huge seaports to be found along the Chinese coast, particularly at Dalian, Tianjin, Shanghai, Ningbo and Huangpu (near Guangzhou). Air links with the outside world are provided by the state-owned airline, CAAC. China is experimenting with new aircraft designs, but at the moment makes use of foreign-made aircraft.

Visiting China

Before 1976 few foreign visitors came to China. 'Friendship Associations' which were sympathetic to socialism organized visits, and they still arrange tours to see schools, factories, hospitals, neighbourhood committees and historical sites. However, after China opened its doors to the west in the late 1970s, commercial tourism boomed, and China has been trying hard to create more facilities for tourists.

Huge hotels, often built by American or Hong Kong-based companies, have sprung up to meet the new demand. They can contribute to the impression gained by some visitors of being on a rather impersonal conveyor belt. At most major sites there are souvenir shops and stalls, sometimes rather tawdry. Foreigners in China are not supposed to use ordinary Chinese money, but use special 'foreign exchange certificates' which are valid only in certain stores. Few visitors are deterred. They find it a fascinating country, with its mixture of ancient tradition and modern experiment in a vast and often extremely beautiful landscape.

▼ A goods train steams past a threshing ground north of Beijing. Coal is mined in northern China and transported great distances by rail. Transport and industrial requirements lead to distribution difficulties, so that southerners usually cannot heat their homes with coal.

40

Transporting goods the old way: these keys are carrying hay along a stretch of old Silk Route which passes through Taklamakan Desert. In the middle ages vans of camels and donkeys carried and 'bricks' of tea to the Middle East Europe.

▲ Not quite the real thing: tourists dressing up as emperors in reproduction Dragon Robes. The Summer Palace, set on hills around a large lake, was built by Ci Xi after the British and French destroyed the original palace nearby in 1860. Today it attracts many tourists.

▼ This double-decker bridge over the Yangzi carries both road and rail. The Nanjing River Bridge was built at speed during the 1960s. When Soviet engineers left the country in 1960, China wanted to show it could manage just as well on its own.

Gazetteer

Beijing (Peking) 39 49N 116 30E
Municipality. pop. *c*9 million. Capital of
China almost continuously since Kublai
Khan's reign in the thirteenth century.
Important rail junction. Iron and steel,
petrochemicals, machine tools, motors,
agricultural equipment, electronics,
chemicals, textiles. Tourist centre: shops,
hotels, restaurants.
Changchun 43 20N 126 30E Pop. *c*2
million. Capital of JILIN province.
Industrial centre on rail junction. Truck
plant, locomotive manufacture, tractors,
pharmaceuticals, rubber tyres, footwear,
tobacco.
Changsha 28 10N 113 10E Pop. *c*3
million. Capital of HUNAN province.
Nearby Shaoshan is birthplace of Mao
Zedong. Heavy and light industry,
foodstuffs, porcelain, cotton.
Chengdu 30 50N 104 5E Pop. *c*4 million
Capital of SICHUAN province. Commercial
centre in fertile Sichuan Basin,
increasingly important for tourism. Food
processing, silk manufacture, textiles,
precision instruments, electronics, timber
processing.
Chongqing (Chungking) 29 32N 106 45E
Pop. *c*7 million. Former Treaty Port at
head of navigable section of the Yangzi
Jiang. Nationalist capital of China
1938–46. Stop-over for tourists. Major
iron and steel manufacturing centre.
Ships, electrical equipment, rolling stock,
plastics, synthetic rubber, cement.
Fuzhou (Foochow) 26 10N 119 20E Pop.
*c*1.5 million. Capital of FUJIAN province.
One of the original Treaty Ports (1842).
Centre for commerce, manufacture and
tourism. Important sea port.
Guangzhou (Canton) 23 15N 113 30E
Pop. *c*6 million. Capital of GUANGDONG
province, situated on Zhu Jiang (Pearl
River). Former Treaty Port (1842). Chief
seaport, industrial and commercial centre
of S. China. Nearby Shenzhen is site of
first 'Special Economic Zone'. Light
industry, paper, cement, chemicals,
textiles, food processing, iron and steel,
machine tools.
Guiyang (Kweiyang) 26 50N 106 55E
Pop. *c*1.5 million. Capital of GUIZHOU
province. Transport centre.
Manufacturing centre. Iron and steel,
machinery, cement, chemicals, aluminium
plant.
Hangzhou (Hangchow) 29 55N 120 15E
Pop. *c*1.5 million. Capital of maritime
province of ZHEJIANG. Former Treaty
Port. Commercial and tourist centre. Silk.
Steel and chemicals.
Harbin 45 40N 126 40E. Pop. *c*2.5
million. Capital of HEILONGJIANG
Province. Former Treaty Port. Important
commercial and industrial centre.

Machine tools, machinery.
Hefei 31 50N 117 0E. Pop. *c*1.5 million.
Capital of ANHUI province. Light
industries moved from Shanghai after
1949. Steel, aluminium, engineering.
Huhehot 40 50N 111 20E Pop. *c*1.5
million. Capital of INNER MONGOLIAN
AUTONOMOUS REGION. Commercial
centre for pastoral economy. Sugar
refinery, diesel engine factory, chemical
fertilizer plant, mineral processing.
Jinan 36 60N 117 0E Pop. *c*3.5 million.
Capital of SHANDONG province. Textiles,
flour, vegetable oil, iron and steel.
Kunming 25 3N 102 40E. Pop. *c*2 million.
Capital of YUNNAN province. Centre of
transport network, on route to Haiphong
in Vietnam before mid 1970s. Machinery,
optical instruments.
Lanzhou 36 0N 109 0E Pop. *c*2.5 million.
Capital of GANSU province. Centre of
transportation network. Chemical and oil
refinery, machinery, fertilizers, rubber and
aluminium, uranium enrichment.
Lhasa 29 42N 91 10E. Pop. *c*0.25 million.
Capital of TIBETAN AUTONOMOUS
REGION (XIZANG). Potala Palace in Lhasa
is the centre of Tibetan Buddhism. The
previous ruler and spiritual leader of
Tibet, the Dalai Lama, has lived in India
since 1959. Some industry, traditional
crafts.
Nanchang 28 22N 115 49E. Pop. *c*2.5
million. Capital of JIANGXI province.
Centre for communications. Food
processing, oil extraction, cotton textiles.
Truck and aircraft production.
Nanjing (Nanking) 32 5N 118 55E. Pop.
*c*4 million. Capital of JIANGSU province.
Former Treaty Port, Nationalist capital of
China 1928–38, 1946–49. River port.
Iron and steel, chemicals, textiles,
agricultural and electrical equipment.
Nanning 22 50N 107 8E. Pop. *c*1 million.
Capital of GUANGXI ZHUANG
AUTONOMOUS REGION. Chemicals,
metallurgical and mining machinery.
Shanghai 31 15N 121 35E. Municipality.
pop. *c*12 million. China's largest city.
Became important as Treaty Port after
Opium War (1842). Very crowded.
Important tourist and cultural centre,
excellent transport connections. Trade
and manufacturing centre. Textiles, steel,
shipbuilding, chemicals, oil refinery,
electrical equipment, motor vehicles,
machine tools.
Shenyang (Mukden) 41 50N 124 0E
Pop. *c*4.5 million. Capital of LIAONING
province, former Treaty Port. Steel,
copper, lead, zinc works. Machinery,
tools, electrical equipment, bicycles,
trams, aircraft. Textiles and chemicals.
Shijiazhuang 38 10N 115 0E Pop. *c*1
million. Capital of HEBEI province.
Railway town. Cotton and woollen mills.
Taiyuan 38 2N 112 20E Pop. *c*1.5
million. Capital of SHANXI (Shansi)
province. Iron and steel, chemicals,
fertilizers, food processing, farm
machinery, textiles.

Tianjin (Tienstin) 39 0N 117 5E.
Municipality. pop. *c*8 million.
Former Treaty Port (1858), has acted
as port for Beijing for 500 years. The
two municipalities border each
other. Clearing house for all
North China's industrial and
agricultural products. Huge port at
Xingang. Steelworks. Engineering,
chemicals, saltworks, electronics,
paper, rubber, agriculture.
Urumchi (Ulumuqi) 44 0N 88 0E Pop.
*c*1 million. Capital of XINJIANG
UIGHUR AUTONOMOUS REGION. Iron and
steel, engineering equipment, chemicals
textiles, tourism.
Wuhan 30 45N 114 15E Pop. *c*4 millio
Capital of HUBEI province. Known as
'Crossroads of nine provinces', it has b
a trade centre for the interior for 500
years. Scene of Wuchang Uprising, 191
Part of it (Hankou) is a former Treaty
Port. Iron and steel, locomotives and
rolling stock.
Xi'an (Sian) 34 0N 109 0E Pop. *c*2.5
million. Capital of SHAANXI (Shensi)
Province. Communciations centre in
midst of important archaeological and
historical area. Tomb of Qin Shihuang,
first emperor of China, nearby. Cotton
and woollen mills, electrical industries,
tractors, porcelain.
Xining 37 0N 102 0E. Pop. *c*1 million.
Capital of QINGHAI province. Iron and
steel, ball bearings, farm tools, electric
equipment, plastics, chemicals, fertilize
Yinchuan 37 0N 106 0E Pop. *c*1 millio
Capital of NINGXIA HUI AUTONOMOUS
REGION, on Huang He. Linen mills,
agricultural products, processing of hic
Zhengzhou (Chengchow) 34 90N 113 1
Pop. *c*1.5 million. Capital of HENAN
province. Textiles, flour mills, oil
extraction, agriculture, tractors,
aluminium.

CHINA IN HISTORY	
Imperial Dynasties	
The Shang	*c* 1480 – 1050
The Zhou	1122 – 221
The Qin	221 – 206
The Han	202 BC – AD 2
The Wei, The Jin, the Northern & Southern	AD 220 – 5
The Sui	586 – 6
The Tang	618 – 9
The Five Dynasties and Ten Kingdoms	907 – 9
The Song	960 – 12
The Liao	960 – 11
The Jin	1115 – 12
The Yuan	1271 – 13
The Ming	1368 – 16
The Qing	1644 – 19
The Republican Period	1912 – 194
The People's Republic of China	1949

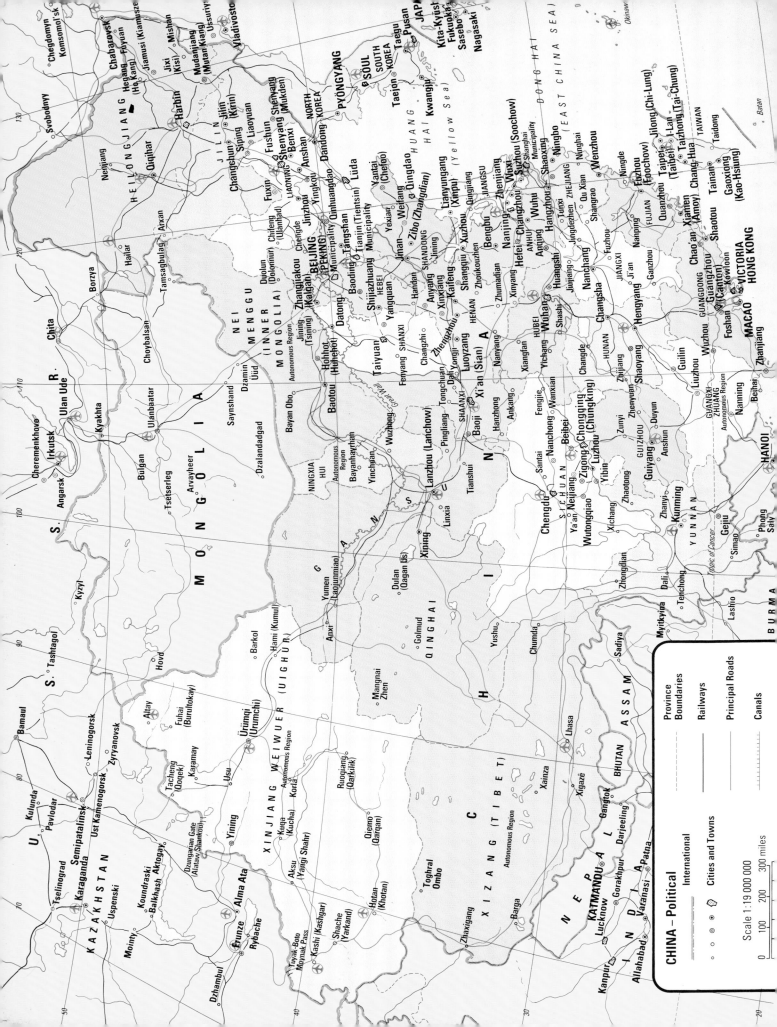

CHINA – Political

	International
o o ⊙	Cities and Towns
	Province Boundaries
	Railways
	Principal Roads
	Canals

Scale 1:19 000 000

0   100   200   300 miles

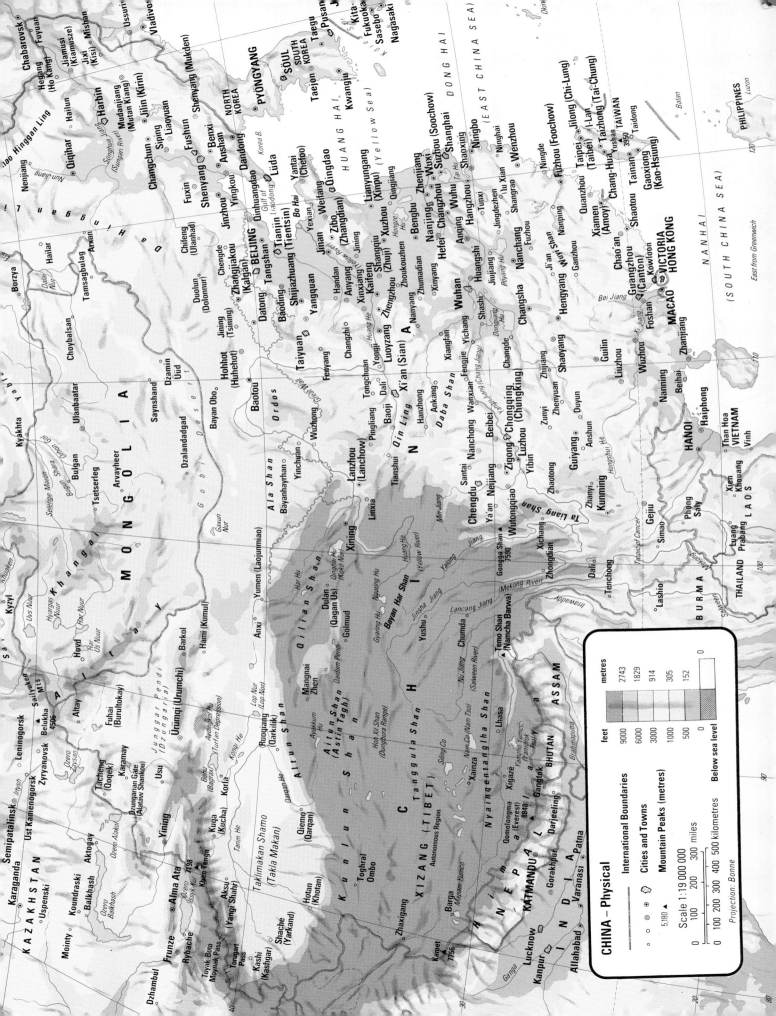

CHINA – Physical